THE SCOOP ON POOP

POOP
Detectives

by Ellen Lawrence

Consultant:

Garret Suen, Assistant Professor
Department of Bacteriology
University of Wisconsin
Madison, Wisconsin

BEARPORT
PUBLISHING

New York, New York

Credits

Cover, © Fat Jackey/Shutterstock, © PHOTO BY LOLA/Shutterstock, and © Mitsuaki Iwago/Minden Pictures/FLPA; 4, © John Eveson/FLPA; 5, © John Eveson/FLPA; 6, © Sinclair Stammers/Science Photo Library; 7, © Vale Stock/Shutterstock; 7T, © Arthur Mustafa/Shutterstock; 8, © Juan Manuel Borrero/Nature Picture Library; 9L, © Michael PotterII/Shutterstock; 9, © Fletcher & Baylis/Science Photo Library; 10, © Working Dogs for Conservation; 11, © Steve Winter/National Geographic Creative; 12, © Biosphoto/Alamy; 13, © Louise Heusinkveld/Alamy; 14T, © Photobank Gallery/Shutterstock; 14B, © UGREEN 3S/Shutterstock; 15, © SCIMAT/Science Photo Library; 16, © Nancy Greifenhagen/Alamy; 17, © Reuters/Alamy; 18, © Nigel Bean/Nature Picture Library; 19, © Kurita Kaku/Getty Images; 20T, © Ancient Southwest Texas Project, Texas State University; 20BL, © Kaiskynet/Shutterstock; 20BR, © Bin Thanh Bui/Shutterstock; 21, © Roy H. Andersen/Getty Images; 22 (L to R), © Sabena Jane Blackbird/Alamy, © Richard Becker/FLPA, © schankz/Shutterstock, and © Lapis2380/Shutterstock; 23TL, © Vladimir Wrangel/Shutterstock; 23TC, © Kenny CMK/Shutterstock; 23TR, © Pressmaster/Shutterstock; 23BL, © Kateryna Kon/Shutterstock; 23BC, © Rich Carey/Shutterstock; 23BR, © didesign021/Shutterstock.

Publisher: Kenn Goin
Senior Editor: Joyce Tavolacci
Creative Director: Spencer Brinker
Photo Researcher: Ruth Owen Books

Library of Congress Cataloging-in-Publication Data

Names: Lawrence, Ellen, 1967– author.
Title: Poop detectives / by Ellen Lawrence.
Description: New York, New York : Bearport Publishing, [2018] | Series: The scoop on poop | Audience: Ages 5–8. | Includes bibliographical references and index.
Identifiers: LCCN 2017014718 (print) | LCCN 2017019438 (ebook) | ISBN 9781684022991 (ebook) | ISBN 9781684022458 (library)
Subjects: LCSH: Animal droppings—Juvenile literature. | Animal behavior—Juvenile literature. | Animal health—Juvenile literature. | Tracking and trailing—Juvenile literature.
Classification: LCC QL768 (ebook) | LCC QL768 .L29 2018 (print) | DDC 591.5—dc23
LC record available at https://lccn.loc.gov/2017014718

For more information, write to Bearport Publishing Company, Inc., 45 West 21st Street, Suite 3B, New York, New York 10010. Printed in the United States of America.

10 9 8 7 6 5 4 3 2 1

Contents

Up Close with Dung

A zoo **veterinarian** is at work in a **lab**.

She opens a large refrigerator and takes out a box.

Is it her lunch? No—the box contains rhino poop!

She scoops out a pea-sized lump and adds it to a bowl of salty water.

Then she begins to examine the poopy water under a **microscope**.

a mixture of poop and water

Vets and other scientists can learn a lot from an animal's poop. At a zoo, keepers collect dung samples for the vets to study. The poop is stored in a refrigerator to keep it fresh.

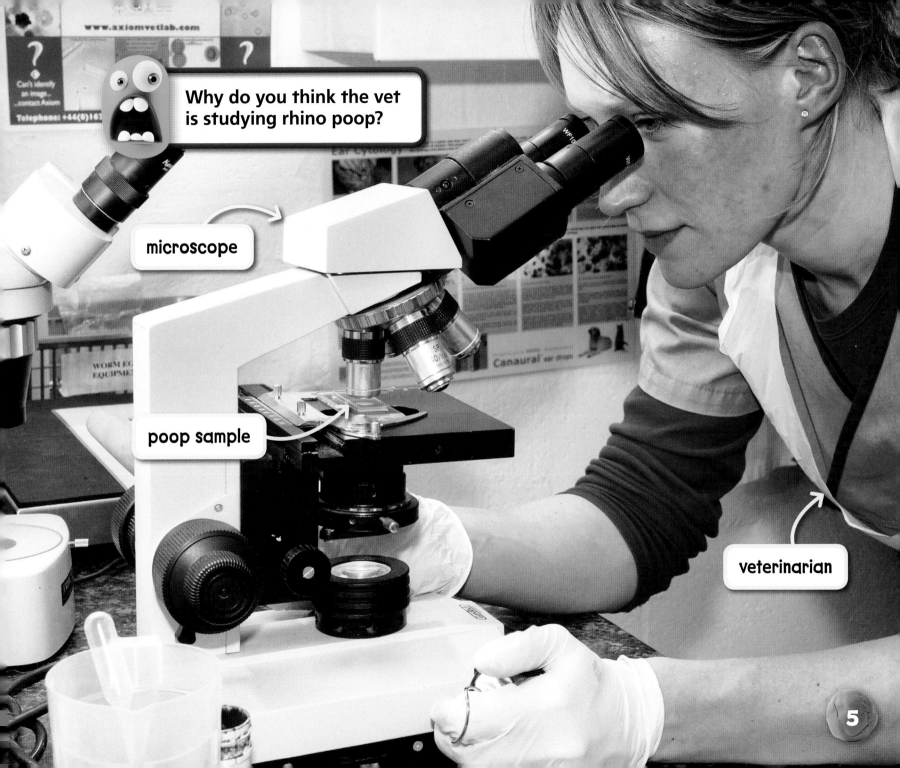

A Poop Checkup

The vet is looking for **parasites**, such as roundworms, that may be living inside the rhino and making it sick.

Roundworms lay their eggs in an animal's stomach.

When the animal poops, the tiny eggs are passed out in its feces.

The vet checks the rhino's dung for worm eggs.

If there are lots of eggs, the rhino needs some worm-killing medicine.

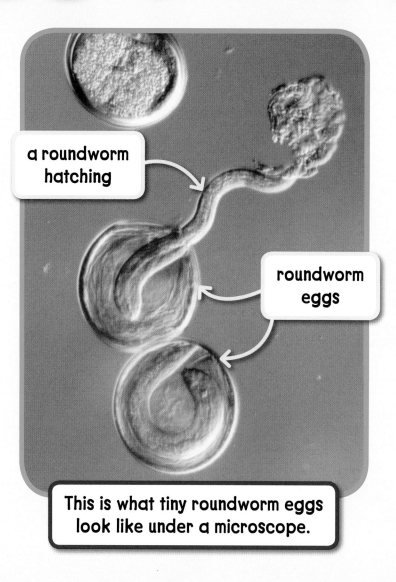

a roundworm hatching

roundworm eggs

This is what tiny roundworm eggs look like under a microscope.

edible glitter

rhino

Sometimes, a zoo vet needs to check the poo of just one animal in a large group. The zookeeper may mix edible glitter with that animal's food, which makes its poo sparkle! That way, the zookeeper can find the right animal's poop.

rhino dung

Endangered Animals

Around the world, many animals are **endangered**.

Scientists can discover a lot about these animals by studying their dung.

They can test the poop for chemicals that show if an animal is hungry, sick, or stressed.

It's not always easy, however, to find a pile of poo in a large forest or field.

So some scientists have furry helpers!

a scientist collecting wolf droppings

scientists measuring elephant dung

Many animals are endangered because their homes have been destroyed. When part of a forest is cut down, where do the animals that once lived there go? Scientists can track them by searching for their dung.

How do you think scientists might find wild animal dung?

Sniffing for Scat

One way to find wild animal poop is by using a dog's super sense of smell!

Some dogs have been trained to sniff for scat, or dung.

Once a scat dog finds some dung, it's rewarded with a game of fetch.

Scat dogs have helped scientists track and study bears, tigers, cougars, and wolves.

The information gathered by these furry poop detectives has been used to help many wild animals.

Wicket the scat dog

Each bag contains a sample of bear poop found by Wicket.

Bruiser the dog finding tiger scat

Scientists can trap endangered animals to study them. However, this can be stressful for the animals. Studying scat is a good way to learn about wild animals without disturbing them.

Doggy Detectives

Amazingly, scat dogs can even find whale poop in the ocean.

The dogs work alongside scientists on boats.

Once a dog picks up a scent, it gives a sign to show the humans which way to turn the boat.

For example, the dog might lean in the direction of the dung.

A specially trained scat dog can smell whale poop from about 1 mile (1.6 km) away!

whale poop floating in the ocean

Whales can be harmed by swallowing oil, chemicals, and other **pollution**. By studying their poop, scientists can discover how ocean pollution is making whales sick.

a scat dog sniffing for whale poop

Why do you think some poop detectives might collect dog doo-doo from a sidewalk?

A Smelly Problem

Have you ever stepped in a pile of dog poop on the street? It's disgusting!

Now scientists are looking into ways to catch owners who don't clean up after their dogs.

Just like all living things, a dog's body and poop contain DNA.

DNA is a special code within the cells of all living things.

Luckily for the poop detectives, no two animals have the same DNA.

This is an illustration of DNA. *DNA* stands for "deoxyribonucleic acid."

This picture was taken using a microscope. It shows tiny bacteria in dog poop.

In addition to DNA, dog poop can contain up to three billion tiny living things called bacteria. Some of these bacteria can cause serious illnesses.

bacteria

Cleaning Up the Streets

How will scientists use DNA to stop the dog poop problem?

In the future, some towns might make all dogs take a DNA test.

The DNA of each animal will then be kept on a computer.

If dog poop is found on the street, scientists can test it for DNA.

Then they'll be able to match the poop to the guilty dog owner!

To gather DNA, a vet wipes a Q-tip inside a dog's mouth. A tiny amount of skin from the mouth sticks to the Q-tip. DNA is collected from this skin and then sent to a lab.

Prehistoric Poop

Did you know that prehistoric poop is useful to scientists, too?

In 2002, scientists found the remains of a giant woolly mammoth in Siberia.

The animal had been buried in the frozen ground for about 22,500 years.

Inside its body, the scientists found dung balls.

After examining the balls, they found out the mammoth's last meal included willow twigs and dead leaves!

mammoth dung

a model of a
woolly mammoth

What time of year did
the mammoth die? The animal
had been eating dead leaves. Also,
the twigs in the poop were starting
to grow new leaves. Using these
clues, the scientists learned that the
mammoth had died in early spring.

Rats and Prickly Pears!

Inside a cave in Texas, scientists have found hundreds of lumps of dried feces.

The ancient poop belonged to people who lived up to 10,000 years ago!

The feces contained bones from fish, birds, lizards, and small rats.

Scientists also found tiny pieces of prickly pear cacti and wild onions.

From learning about ancient people to helping animals, scientists discover plenty from poop!

prehistoric human feces

wild onions

prickly pear